For my beautiful niece Esther who kept giggling and kept me giggling long enough to finish this book for my wonderful grand children Millie, Ruben and Joshua to discover and giggle their way through too.

And thanks to all the other gigglers who helped along the way.

first printed Feb 2017

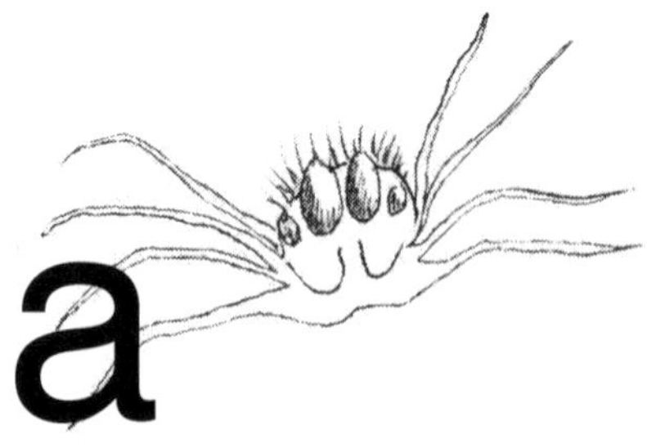

acclaimed arachnid alvin arranges aromatic
aerosols

an accomplished artist
alvin's amazing achievements
astounded acquaintances

another ability
amplifying astral anomalies
affected an average afternoons ambling
around an african appliquéd armchair

absorbing aerial ambience
and adjusting antenna alignment
alvin accidentally accesses an alien
announcement

an amplified acid-house arrangement
absolutely achieving atmosphere

an alien assemblage announced abruptly

all arachnids are absolutely affronted

and appalled about atrocious antisocial acrid
airborne aromas

ahhhhhhh..... abduction

astonished alvin appears aboard

amidst astrometric arrays and arrogant
anchovies acrobatic aracnitoids argue about
audacious apricots

acknowledging alvin
administrator arsilla approaches
applying almond atomiser around abundantly
ample armpits and attaching appropriate
accessories

after admiring alvin's assorted appendages
arsila apologizes and awkwardly admits
abandoning alvin accidentally around
accrington ages ago

apologies aside
after accelerating across astronomical areas
avoiding apocalyptic antelopes
annihilating abominable anal acoustics

an apparition appears
an arachnid

an artist
an advantageous alliance

any aromatic aerosols available

alvin although astounded
already anticipated arsilas amorous attempts
at amassing aerologic artefacts

answered
alas
aren't any available
all atomized
actually all ablutionary acts are abolished

anyway
alternative arrangements
august appointments
aerosol association
applique

adieu
and adios amigos
an amorphous aperture appears
around an adjacent aluminium atrium

alvin's abdominal apparatus activates an abhorrent aroma

agile alvin abseils away

audacious apricots attached

b

bertram barnacle

baked.

broiled bottoms

belching beverages

besides belligerent brews

but before breakfast beloved bertram

balancing beautifully

(buttocks bulging between bejewelled bikini)

boldly begins breathtakingly brilliant ballet

bewitching besotted bystanders beyond belief

binkie

bertram's butler
briskly brings blueberry blancmange because

broiled bottoms

blimey

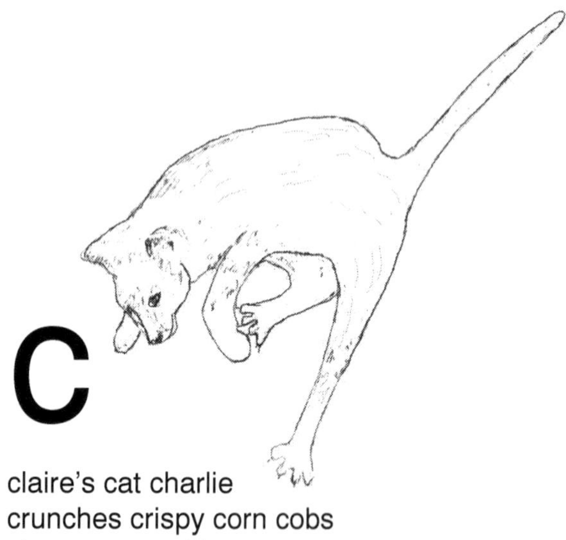

C

claire's cat charlie
crunches crispy corn cobs
chases crocodiles

cautiously
comically

charlie cleans cadillac cars
commercially
counts countless computers

consistently
charmingly

cunningly changes counterfeit currency
confidently checks corned chicken's
consistency

cleverly
creatively

charlie's chum
claire's camouflaged cat
creatively crochets cabbage coloured caps
concocts cakes containing custard cream
cheese
curiously catapults curved Chimpanzees

concentrically
carefully

come champion cats
communicates claire
clambering charlie calls camouflaged chum

cheerfully
chirpily

choosing comfy couch cushions confidently

close cherished companions

cuddle contentedly

d

during dewy days
dazzling diamanté dew drops drip

distinguished dandelions dancing dreamily
drink dappled daylight

derek dilly dallies
daily delighting
deadheading
dibbing
dividing digitalis
deliberating
dawdling

distressed derek detects
dreaded
despicable
dandelions

dam
double dam

derek distinctly disturbed
digs deep

dispatching dozens
dredging dusty dirt dementedly
dragging destroying

dratted dandelions

destruction
devastation

downright
disgraceful

derek
depleted
diminished
drops defeated

discerning dandelions
dauntlessly discover deserted ditches
derelict districts
different domains
diligently dispersing drifter descendants
distributing defiantly down deeply dipping
dingley dells

e

ernestine envisioned entertaining everyone

except
ernestine's extreme emanations
elicited enragement

early evening
eerily evil exploding emissions emanated

evolving exponentially

effectively eclipsing everything

eventually
ernestine's embarrassing episode eased

everybody else expired entirely

emancipated

ernestine enthusiastically erupted
expelling epitaphs epitomizing erstwhile
expiree's

ethereally echoing eternally

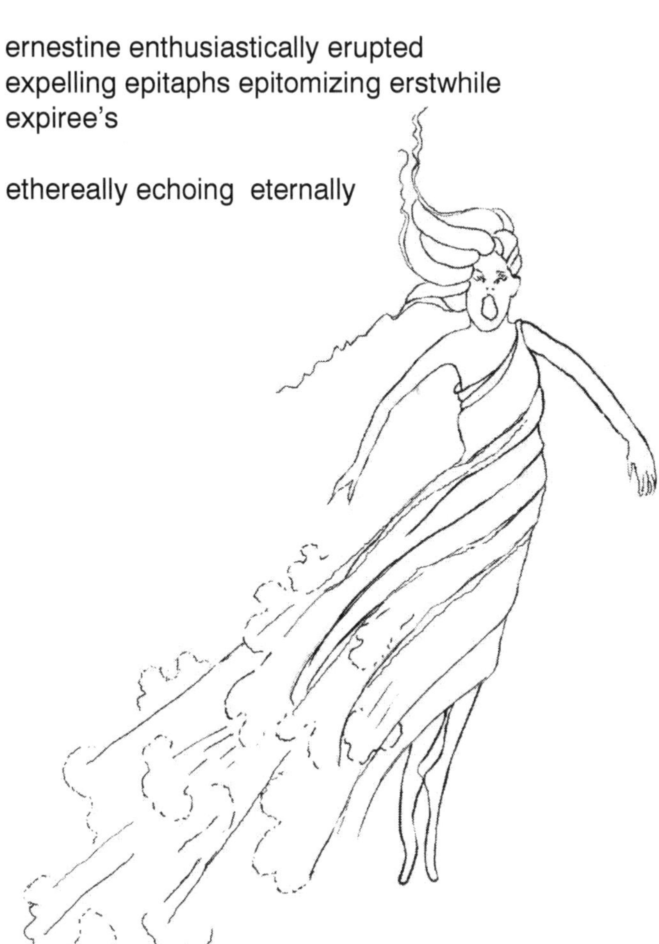

flo foolishly flipped for finkish fin
famous five footed footballer from frome

fleetingly fin flatters flo
(fiendish fink forges fivers)

friday's football final follows
five frog faced fans fly flags
french fleas fry fish flavoured flapjacks

flo floats flawlessly

fanning four fragrant flippers
frank (freckles) fine fourteen foot fandango
freak
fancies flo
fin flirts with freda

flo frets
flak follows
flippers fly

feisty frank fixes fraudulent fin
fin flounders

flibbertigibbet
flashes flo

fortuitous fluke for formidable frank
flooring fin finds flo's favour

frank faces flo fondly
flo's fetching fluorescent frock fluttered
frank's fandango flowed fantastically
finally flo fell for frank

g

gallant green gherkins go galloping gaily
gauntlets glinting go go go
gambling
gleefully goading greta
ginormous gorgon (genghis grunt)

grumpy greta
gets grotty gumboils
guzzles goats
grows ginger gloops

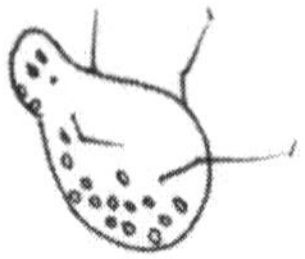

generously girthed grouchy greta
gnawing gingham galoshes growls
gruffly go go get going
gelatinous gadabouts
greta's grotto glistens golden
ghostly grasses gently gleam

greta glimpses gherkins grieving
grimly gasping gloomily
garbled grumbles gushing glibly
gherkins gesture glaringly

grinding gadgets
gouging gashing

gardeners gumboots
gungy grime
grasping gently greens growing
gravely gifting gullied ground

glowering ginormous greta
generates ghoulish growls
gormless gardeners glaring grovel
grapple gawping
going gone

greta gathers gloomy gherkins
goodness gracious
giddy gumdrops
go gamble
graze
go go go

greta grimaces growling gently

giggling green gherkins go galloping gaily

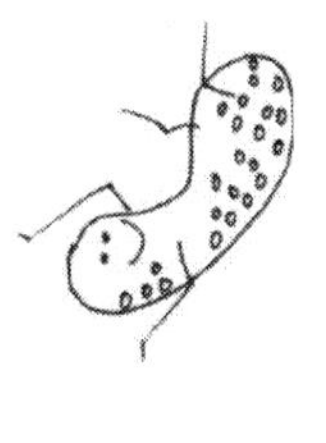
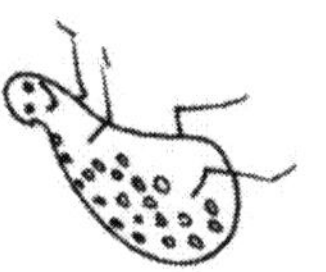
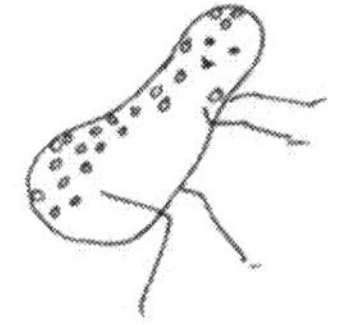
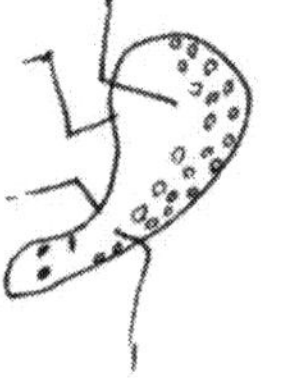

hens herd hedgehogs
honestly

hens hushed hypnotic harmonising
helps hasten hedgehogs happy hibernations

here is head honcho hakeem's harem

harem
ha ha
hilarious
hazel hen howls
hannah heckles
hefty hattie hoiks his hammock

hakeem
hardly

hakeem hops happily hugging hattie's head

however hakeem's harem have hankerings
hot holidays
handbags

high heels
hashish

hiking holiday
hints hakeem

hiking holiday

hollers hattie hooting

hawaii

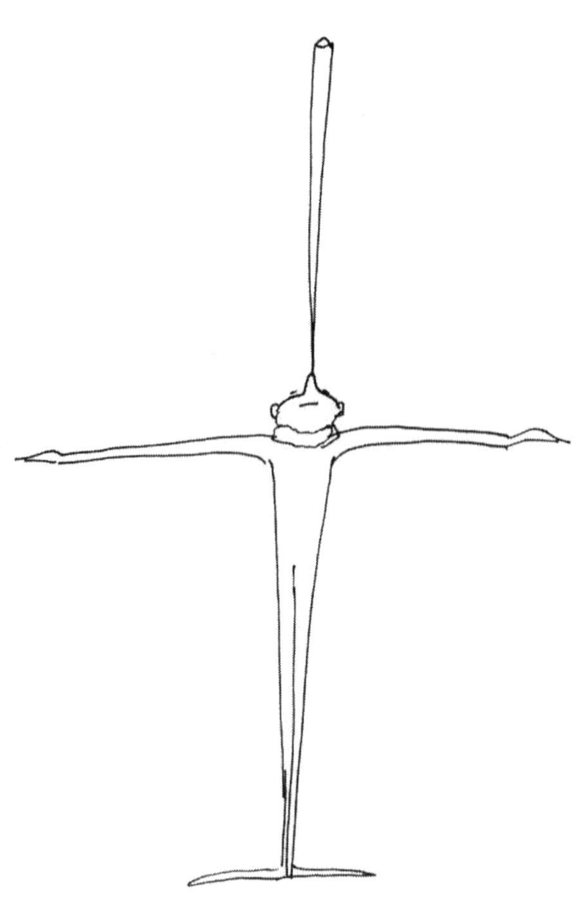

i

inuit ivor insisted
icicles improved imagination
incrementally

incrementally
ice
impossible
interjected irene

insulted
ivor indignantly inched into insignificance

j

jolly jumbo jets
jiggle jovially
jabber joyfully
jump jive jubilantly

juvenile jets join jostling
jamming jauntily

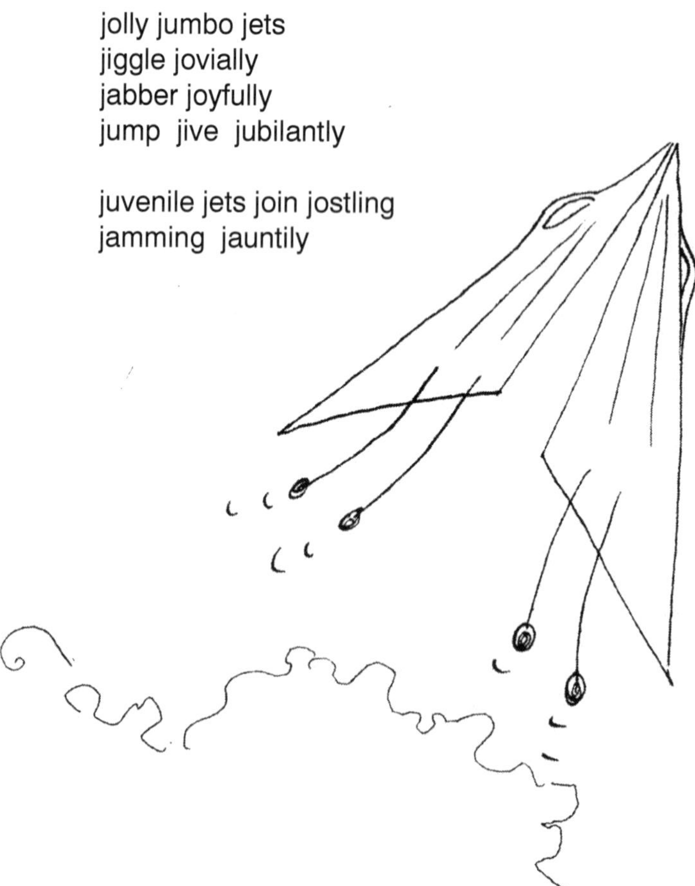

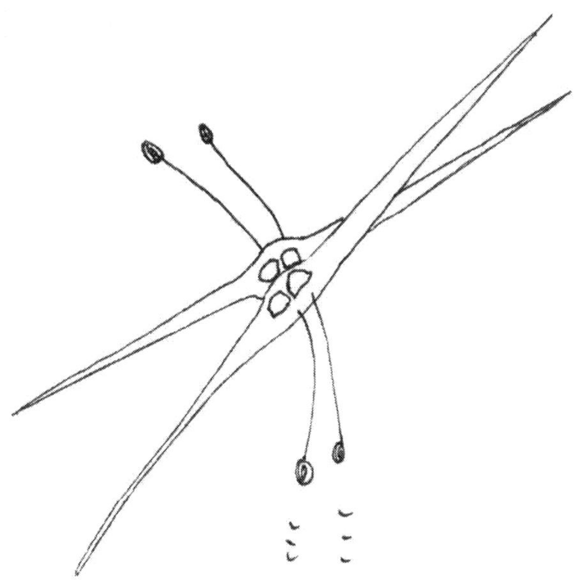

just judicious jazz jack
just judicious jazz

k

kippers
keep
kicking
kai's *
knees

*kai = ocean

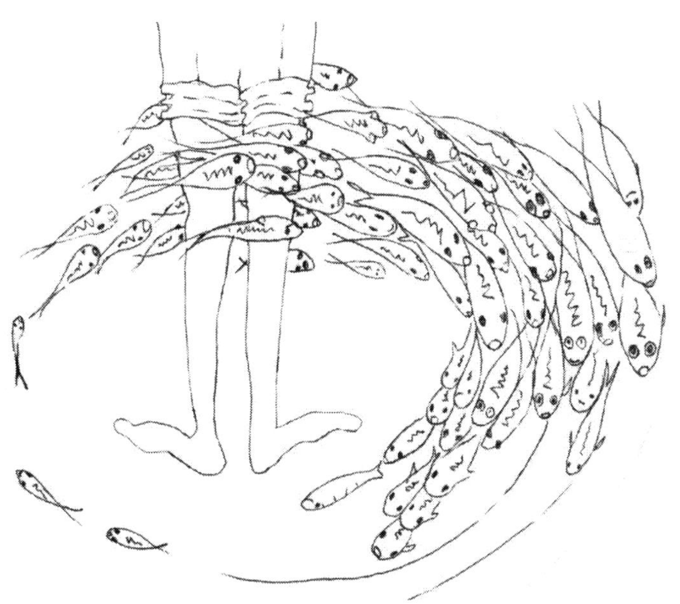

l

loretta lamoure

(larry)

loves lists

long lists

lovingly logged lists

lists like

listing

lingerie

like leatherette

lacy lycra leggings

lavish lamé leotards

leopard look latex loungewear

laying listed lingerie lightly

loretta laden lingers

lastly

luscious lips lilac lipstick

later

leather luggage labelled

loretta lamoure

looking like larry

limbers lively

light loafers laced
linen lapels lifted.

leaves london

laughing loudly

lookout lanzarote
lorettas landing

most majors mend mirrors

many manipulate marsh mallows
making miniature monkeys

maybe more meet melancholy meteorites
meticulously measuring miniscule molluscs

marshalling malicious monsters

memorizing meaningful moments

mentally milking mammoths

my major mumbles melodically
minding my mouse

n

n'er-do-wells never nuzzle noses
nincompoops nominally note
naturally nostrils need nurture
nubby noses need nips
neat noses need nothing
nevertheless
noses need nice niffs

nutritional nosegays
nectar
no noxious nappy niffs
nothing nauseous nor nuclear
noses need nice niffs

neglected noses nurture
nasty nodding nodes
narrowing nearby nostrils
negatively numbing nerves

nebulous noselings nestle
near numerous naturalised nooks
notorious nematodes nibble
nefarious newts nip

nevertheless
noses need nice niffs

now
noisy nasal nightmares
no noble nozzle

nits

nonsensically noseless

needed nicer niffs

O

oh opulent owl of our old oak
omnipotent occasionally odd
owner of obsidian ocular orbs
oh one of only one

omnipresent outstanding owl
overtly ostentatious owl
oscillating orienteering owl
oh one of only one

pigeons poo purposely
particularly pursuing pedestrians

pin point precision performed perfectly
part provocation

people puzzle pigeons
perversely polluting places
pouring poisonous preparations
pestilence plagues

people popularly portray pigeons
possessing primitive paltry personalities

preposterous

predominantly principled professionals
pigeons primarily promote positive possibilities

professor peony peck
particle physicist
pronounces
pooing proves pivotal

pauses

proliferating planetary propagation processes

psychic petunia peck
plumage preened
precariously perched
prophesises portentous prospects

pubescent progeny precocious
peter peck
pursues policemen
practicing particularly potent purging

pickled poppa peck
preeminent psychiatrist
provides powerful pineapple punch

people present poor psychological
programming

pity

q

quarrelsome
queen
quoot
quizzed
quirkily
quaint
quadruped
quentin

quentin
quickly
quoted
quality
quips

quincy's
quartet
quietly
quaked
quivering
quavers

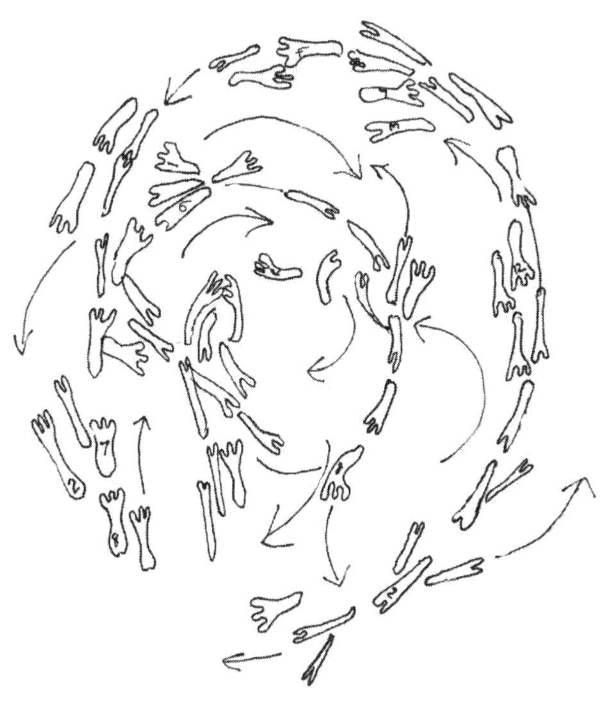

quentin's
quality
quickstep
quickly
quashed
queen
quoot's
quibbles

rancorous rodents retreat

reinvigorate relationships - run riot

reasonable rates

rumpus rooms

rubbish rummaging - rabble rousing

ransacking

renowned recipes

reeking relish - rank roulade

rat racing

rotund rodents rigorous reducing

revelations

renowned rodents regale raucous raids

roundtables

reviewing rudimentary rewiring

remedies

removing roundworms

re-emerge rejuvenated replete

residents regulations

reprehensible reprobates regurgitating roommates
result - robust removal – relationship revoked
reimbursement refused

relatives requesting redress require recent relevant
recognizable remains

retrospective requests rejected.

S

sponsors
slick slugs sign steals substantial stage space
stating
slick slugs solution stimulates sluggish slime

silver suited slug steve speaks
(scripted)
so
snoring symposium season seven
sincere salutations staunch snoring stalwarts

stage superbly set
sumptuous sofas satin sheets
scrumptious strawberries
sensational super stars
specifically

stunning sarina snot

servants strategically
supervise serena's stage show
smoke swirls
serena sashays
sequined stiletto shoe sparkling
shamelessly she sports sheer skimpy skirts

spellbound spectators scream

serena serena serena

syncopated saxophones swing
steve shouts

super slinky snood sisters

stella snood saunters seductively
slowly she starts shimmying

simultaneously
sleek sibling saliva snood
slithers sinuously
scandalously scanty silk scarfs
selected specifically
send shockwaves

shivered spines skyrocket

suddenly

senile sap
shouts serena

spillage
screams saliva

stella sipping sangria sways

supporters skilfully steer sozzled stella
she slurs
strumpets

standards slugs standards
seething saliva squelches stella's shoe

such shenanigans

serenading sirens start singing softly
slippers slipped
snuggling snoozing superstar slugs
sleep

soon snooting snorts soar

star struck spectators sigh

spikes start swishing sideways straining the
snorometer

several (swiftly seized) snail saboteurs shout
seditious shell slogans

surprisingly
super star slugs slumber soundly

steve summarises

such scandal
skirmishes
saboteurs
shocking

so
serena
stella
saliva

stay seated
supreme snoring slug selection
starts soon

twenty twelve troublesome turquoise tadpoles
tormented thirteen tricky tarantulas
together they tried tasting tea

touching their twinkling tin tea pot twice
they transported themselves to texas
telling tall tales till tuesday

then travelling through turbulent transylvania
they tried tying toast to their toes
totally trapping ten terrible twin tailed tics

taking them through time
they treated the total troupe to trifle

thinking
thursday treacle topped tart tonight

terrific

u

umpteen unloved umbrellas
undergo unrelenting umbrage underwater

unseeing unctuous underlings
unconcerned users

using undeniable unction
umbrellas unite
uploading unnoticed unto unique unparalleled
universes

undiscovered
unshackled
underneath undulating undergrowth

unconventional umbels

utter utopia

V

virtuoso violinist vivian
values victors vibrato voice

victor
vivian’s valentine
visits vast venues

vacuous vulture vince
vivian’s valet,
venerates vivian
veritable varlet

venomous vapours visit victor’s villa
victor vanishes
vamoose

vivian very vexed

vince

vince visibly vacant vacillates

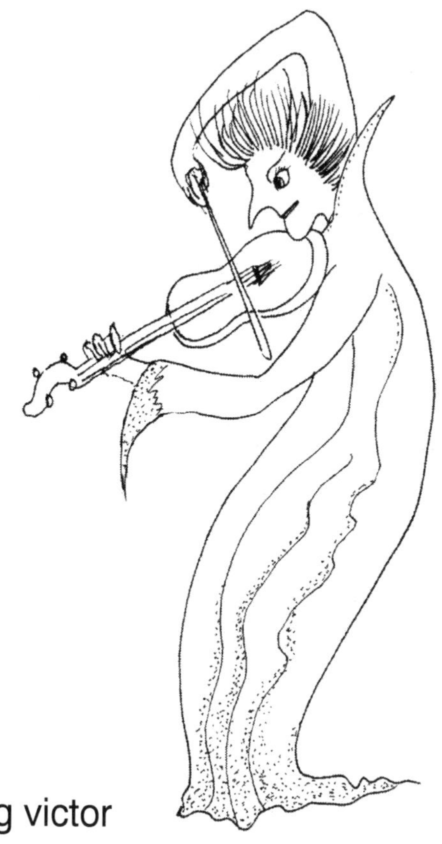

vaporising victor

victor visited vast venues
very valuable venues
vital virtuoso violinist venues

wow wednesday
wizard
wisteria wimple wrapped warm watermelon
within whiffy wellies
well
wednesdays wacky weather worsened

wailing winds whisked wayward weasels
westward
whales wept whilst weaving worsted wondering
why why why

woodpeckers washing weevils with winceyette
wine wondered
why why why

why why why would wildebeests worship
witless willie waddle
why we wonder

wisteria wearing waxed wispy wings
whooshed
windsurfing wonderfully
whilst warbling wildly

we were wondering wisteria
why wildebeests
worship witless willie waddle

whispering widdle who
what warped waffle
why why why
would wildebeest
worship whittling wally whatsit

wierdo's

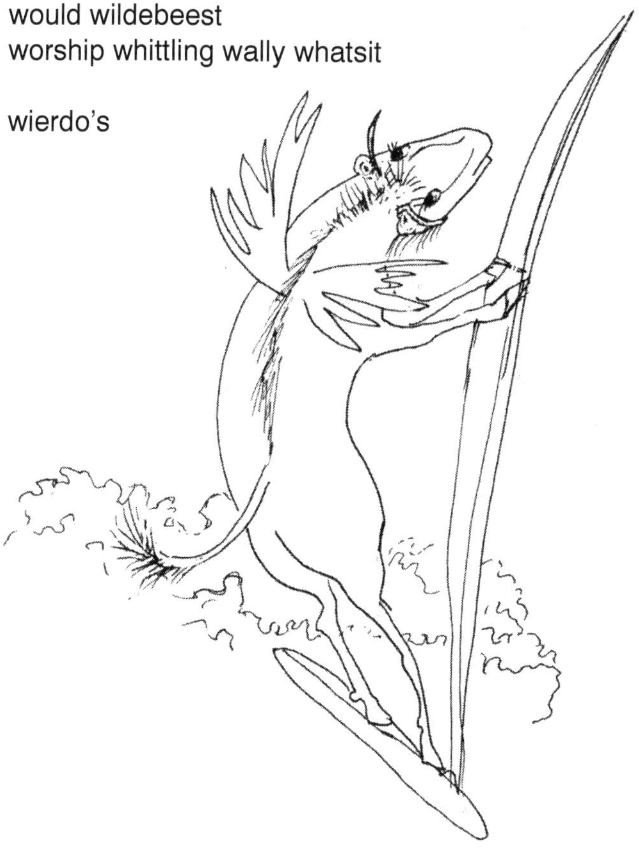

xanthia xenopus*

x-rays

xylophones

*tongueless african frog

y

yo yannis

your yellow yaks yodel

yodel

yes

yipes

your young yaks yonder

yelling

yummy yams

yep

yahoo

yahoo

yearly

yet yesterday

yelled yippy

yogurt

yogurt

yes yaks yearn yogurt

yea

yogurt

yuck

Z

zany
zebra
zephaniah
zoomed
zapping
zig zag
zips
zealously

Printed in Great Britain
by Amazon